TEND
TO IT

A Holistic Guide to Intentional Productivity

Kate Litterer, PhD

www.thetendingyear.com

ISBN 978-1-7358022-0-6 (paperback)
ISBN 978-1-7358022-1-3 (ebook)

Book design and cover design by TK Palad

First Edition

For my Sweetheart, Kris,
who has supported my curious dreams since day one.

Contents

Foreword

Hello! I am Dr. Kate Litterer, a Productivity Coach, researcher, and author. You may have met me through my blog, *The Tending Year* (thetendingyear.com), which documents my experiments with productivity and personal development practices and tools. Or, you may have heard my podcast interviews with Kate Snowise on Here to Thrive, Yarrow Magdalena on The DIY Small Business Podcast, and Anna Joy on The Queer Witch Podcast.[1] Regardless of where and when we met, digitally or face-to-face, I am so pleased that you found your way to *Tend to It: A Holistic Guide to Intentional Productivity*.

I came to study productivity because I was a chronically ill, workaholic, recovering alcoholic who used my intellectual work as a distraction, a coping mechanism, and a way to feel good or bad about myself instead of acknowledging that my worth was not tied to my productivity. I've written before about how my experience with workaholism feels similar to my experience with alcoholism: the switch in my brain that should tell me when I am sated, when to put the bottle down or shut the laptop, never seemed to activate no matter how much I drank or worked.[2]

I hit my alcoholic rock bottom and stopped drinking in March of 2013, and it was the most important decision I have ever made. But even though I thrived in my sobriety from alcohol, I avoided addressing my workaholism. Work was a part of my identity. It was woven into the way I approached life, beginning with receiving praise for getting good grades in elementary school and following me through working multiple jobs at a time to cover rent, bills, and to pay off debt. Decades after I earned gold stars on spelling quizzes, I nestled into the workaholic culture of graduate school, where doing the bare minimum doesn't earn you fellowships, publications, or awards.

Looking back now with awareness and compassion, I can see how my family, teachers, friends, and I all unwittingly subscribed to a bootstrapping mentality that perpetuates a white supremacist and patriarchal obsession with perfectionism.[3] Although I didn't have that language at the time to describe why I acted as I did, I remember how I felt. I feared anything less than perfection because I valued myself not for being, or even for trying, but only for accomplishing.

Healing from this mentality is what shapes my approach to productivity. My research on the "traditional" methods of productivity has shown me that standardized, pre-baked instructions and tools often feed into workaholism and a flattened identity based on production. Additionally, most of the productivity lessons I've learned through my research and practice apply to business, where the focus is on increasing income under a capitalist system, and the assumed reader is often the boss who assigns the labor—not the laborer. The tenets of productivity that circulate in business tomes demand actions like getting to your desk before the sun rises. While strict rules like that may be useful for increasing margins, they can also suck out your soul and wreck your body.

After considering many subtitles for this book, A Holistic Guide to Intentional Productivity emerged as most authentic to my approach to reimagine productivity through the lenses of slow and intentional living (or what I like to call "slowductivity"). My holistic guide shows how to utilize various productivity tools and theories in new ways that can enable us to accomplish our goals while also valuing, conserving, and redirecting our personal resources (time, energy, focus, etc.) towards self-loving practices. Similarly, an intentional approach to productivity privileges setting boundaries around work so that we can prioritize rest, relationships, and personal development just as much as, if not more than, our work.

My Personal Productivity Journey

What happens when you physically, emotionally, or mentally can't meet capitalistic productivity standards?

I would likely have kept up my fear-induced-workaholism had I not developed chronic pain and illness. In January 2017, I signed up for spin classes and quickly became obsessed. I was delighted with my new hobby, but the repetitive impact of the exercise combined with my own propensity to push myself to my limit to hit a personal record awoke a severe and mysterious pain in my sacrum and back. Within the next year, I developed fatigue and symptoms of an autoimmune disorder, and I was finally diagnosed with a form of borrelia similar to Lyme disease in 2020.

But let's rewind to the spring of 2017 when my pain forced me to make significant changes. I was livid, but I was also terrified—because sitting meant pain, and standing also led to pain, and pain meant I couldn't work as "optimally" as I had before. When I read my output as suboptimal, I blamed myself and fell into a pit of self-shaming anger.

Without a diagnosis or answers from my doctors, I turned to personal development podcasts and books as a way to practice being kinder and more loving to myself—my new self that required rest, compassion, and softness. I eventually learned from various podcast hosts that time management tools and boundaries around my technology use could help me feel more relaxed. Whether it's my Gemini moon that craves new knowledge or my comfort with the cause-and-effect properties of tools and how-to guides, I soon found myself researching, experimenting with, and synthesizing my experience with personal productivity on *The Tending Year*. I hoped that my readers would benefit from my distillation of tools through my subjective experience as a chronically ill recovering workaholic.

After four years of consistent research and practice, I'm a successful Productivity Coach and I have earned my doctorate. I'm still chronically ill and sometimes experience pain flares. At the same time, I've developed a rich Iyengar yoga practice, fulfilled my decades-long dream to experiment with watercolors, and I purchased my first violin with a plan to learn how to play the songs Sherlock Holmes played in the novels and short stories. All that is to say, I continue to spin many plates—although fewer than before. Many of the plates I spin are motivated by curiosity and intention, rather than the fearful, workaholic obsession I experienced years ago.

That's what led me to write this book. I want to teach you some of the tools, practices, and approaches that led me to this point so you can develop your own personal productivity practices in a way that fits your current lived experience. No matter where you are right now on your journey—if you feel overwhelmed, exhausted, or stuck, or if you feel curious, ready to go-go-go, or energized (or some combination of both)—this book is for you.

How to Get the Most Out of *Tend to It*

This book covers four key topics that I have found most essential in developing my own productivity practice: **habits, goals, focus,**

and boundaries around my work and technology. I have dedicated a chapter to each topic, where I combine research-based education with various tools, practices, and approaches, and I offer examples throughout the chapters that you can use as models for your own practice. Beyond guiding you through the topics and tools, I also weave tangible exercises and activities within each chapter, which will enable you to put the lessons you learn to practical use *while* you're moving through the book.

In terms of progressing through the text, there are multiple options. You might want to read the book to learn the content without completing any exercises and then complete them on a second read. Or, you might dive right in and complete the activities as you go. Or, you might be drawn to a particular topic, and you can open directly to that chapter when needed. Go with your preference, and know that the activities are scaffolded to build on one another.

How to Get Started

To complete this book, you need to do two things: read and write. You can choose to read, highlight, and dogear the pages of a print version of the book, or you can download the e-book version to a tablet or computer and read it digitally. The book will ask you to complete multiple exercises, and you should feel free to use a notebook or computer document to write or type your answers. Because the book exercises will ask you to refer to your previous answers, I encourage you to write the exercise number in your notebook or document when you complete each activity. The best part of *Tend to It* is that you can repeat the exercises over and over for your future goals, so you can fill a new notebook or document for each goal you take on.

While I use the tools and practices in this book to develop habits, set goals, and focus on my work as a writer and researcher, this book will be helpful to anyone who is working on a project that requires them to make progress across multiple working sessions. So, if you're an artist, a writer, a teacher, a business owner, a fitness instructor, a coach, a stay-at-home-parent, an herbalist, a student, or other vocation-haver or hobby-practicer, I implore you to approach these tools with an intention to make them fit your *own* approach and practice. You may find new, creative, fun ways to accomplish goals, regardless of your profession or your experience with personal productivity.

Building Your Own Personal Productivity

We are constantly shown messages that purport there's one right way to find success, and we are bombarded with tips to get there quicker than everyone else. Even though social media and advertisements would have us think otherwise, practices like productivity, creativity, entrepreneurship, and personal development are not one-size-fits-all. To find what works best for you as an individual, you need to experiment.

During coaching sessions, I emphasize the act of experimenting. I want each of my clients to try out different methods and tools, and then, after reflection, to take, leave, adjust, and improve their individual practices to fit their real lives. There are several reasons why I encourage clients to re-see the act of improving our lives as many small experiments. First and foremost, many prepackaged tools and methods often don't account for the vast differences in people's access, abilities, preferences, and values. When we receive a generalized guarantee that a tool will work for everyone, we can feel like there's something wrong with us if it doesn't work at first (or at all). When we re-see trying tools and methods as experiments that we can later hone or dismiss, we remove the option of "failing."

The tools, practices, and approaches in this book are meant to guide and assist you, and each one can be personalized and adapted. You should approach each tool as an experiment, with an intention to practice the method and hone it so it works for you as an individual. For the purposes of this book, let's imagine experimentation includes:

- Reading about new tools, approaches, and practices so you can grasp how they work on a conceptual level.

- Choosing which tool, approach, or practice you want to try out.

- Identifying a task that you'd like to work on during your experiment.

- Setting a timeframe to conduct your experiment.

- Experimenting with the tool, approach, or practice to work on the task.

- Reflecting on your experience during the experiment.

Reflection is important because it enables you to track your patterns, identify what works best for you, and tweak, edit, or discard the practices that don't fit your particular needs or interests. As you complete the 21 exercises in this book, reflect on how the practices make you feel. Do they make you feel confident? Cool! If trying them leaves you feeling confused or stressed out, please feel free to adapt and evolve them to fit *your* preferences and needs. If you decide that a tool or approach isn't for you, please do not feel like you "have" to use it anyways. Your personal productivity toolkit should enable you to feel confident by prioritizing your strengths, preferences, and skill set. It is completely normal for a person's priorities to shift and change across their life, project, or even an individual task.

If there's one thing that sets me apart from other productivity researchers and coaches, it's my skepticism of a "one-way-only" application of a tool. Our lives are rich and complex, and as a result, our personal productivity will ebb, flow, and require us to personalize which tools, practices, and approaches we use, as well as how, when, and where we use them. I'm honored that you chose me to guide you through that process.

Introduction:
Productivity is Political and Personal

B efore we dive into the research and exercises, I want to have a frank conversation about productivity. Each of us approaches our productivity with various levels of comfort, interest, privilege, and access. We do this within a culture of productivity that has traditionally encouraged treating our bodies like robots that should be able to meet a standard quota—or even worse, suggests that we should compete with one another for a few coveted spots at the top that include their own parking spot and a swimming pool on the roof. Those approaches present productivity as always doing more-more-more, when, by definition, **productivity simply means completing the tasks we intend to complete.**

Productivity as a concept can be beneficial when adapted to each person's goals and tasks. However, what I call Productivity Culture™, or the culture of perfectionism and obsession with standard definitions of "success," can be problematic. When we view productivity as a depoliticized action or assume everyone is seeking the same standards of accomplishment, we ignore the fact that our cultural obsession with perfectionism is rooted in institutionalizing systems of oppression. Productivity does not occur in a vacuum, and it is absolutely tied to access, privilege, white supremacy, classism, and ableism.

I'll use my experience as an example. I am a white, formerly working-class/currently middle-class, chronically ill, cisgender, sober, self-employed, queer femme. I have three graduate degrees, an MFA, an MA, and a PhD, and I live with my partner in a rented townhouse outside of Boston, Massachusetts in the United States. My access to and experience with education and employment is a result of privileges associated with my race, my class, my body that appears on the surface to be able-bodied, my "feminine" gender presentation, the letters after my name, and my access to a home where I can run my own business out of my private home office. I am well researched in productivity, personal development, and slow living, and as a result, I have honed a practice that enables me to be incredibly efficient while working fewer hours than I used to work.

My experience with productivity is limited to the identities I listed above, so I would like to highlight and recommend a short list of writers who study and publish on the experiences of Black, Indigenous, and People of Color (BIPOC) and people with different class and ability experiences to me. This list includes Tricia Hersey, Rachel Cargle, Leah Lakshmi Piepzna-Samarasinha, and adrienne maree brown. To learn more about the ways rest is a political statement and action for BIPOC, please read the writing of Tricia Hersey, the creator of The Nap Ministry (@thenapministry on Instagram). You can read a longer list of recommended reading and listening materials at the end of this book.

Getting Started: Redefining Failure and Success When it Comes to Your Goals

Now that I have touched on accessibility and politicization of productivity, I'd like to discuss goal setting. Goals should motivate us and make us feel good, but it's easy to feel like not accomplishing a goal means we are failures. While this is not true, our brains think it is. Whenever we set a goal, we imagine what it would feel like to achieve that goal. We can actually receive hits of dopamine just by imagining ourselves in our ideal futures where we have achieved our goals. Not only this, but our brains tend to link how good we will feel when we complete our goals with our identities and our views of ourselves. So, when we don't meet our goal as we envisioned we would, we feel as if we have failed ourselves or lost something very dear to us. We grieve the loss of our goals.[4]

I asked myself and friends the question, "Why do you struggle to accomplish your most sought-after goals?" Here's a list of our answers:

- I don't know where to start.
- I am not sure what is really required/involved.
- I am overwhelmed by there not being one set path on how to achieve my goal.
- I can't focus.
- I don't know what a finished project should look like.
- I want to overachieve.
- I feel bored with the project.
- I am tired.
- I struggle to finish a project once I start it.
- I self-sabotage making progress because I fear failing.
- I have imposter syndrome about my ability to do a good job.

Now that you've read the list I compiled, it's time for your first exercise.

Exercise 1:
Why Do I Struggle to Accomplish My Goals?

Write a list in your notebook or document of the reasons why you struggle to accomplish your own goals. If you identify with any of the statements I shared on the previous list, feel free to use them in your list.

Taking the time to brainstorm a list of your personal challenges when it comes to completing goals will enable you to write a more applicable goal setting plan. If you already know your list of struggles, you can reverse engineer your approach to help you navigate potential pitfalls or obstacles.

Let's move on from your list of struggles or challenges to examine your current relationship with habits, goal setting, focus, and setting boundaries around your technology use or any other aspect of your work. I encourage you to include things on your list for Exercise 2 that feel good and motivating as well as feelings of confusion, disappointment, or other challenging experiences.

Exercise 2:
My Current Relationship with My Habits, Goals, Focus, and Boundaries

To complete this exercise, answer the following questions about your relationship with your productivity practices by writing in your notebook or document. Include examples as evidence, and feel free to replace the word "relationship" with "experience" if that feels more concrete to you.

- My current relationship with my habits is...
- My current relationship with my goals is...
- My current relationship with focus is...
- My current relationship with setting boundaries around my work/technology use/etc. is...

Here are some example answers to get you started: "My current relationship with my habits is: I have the best intention to start new practices, but I end up forgetting to do them" or "My current relationship with setting boundaries around my work is: I feel guilty saying no to any potential source of income, so I tend to overbook myself."

Imagining Your Ideal Day

One of my favorite activities is imagining what my ideal fill-in-the-blank would be. Ideal day, wedding, dinner, book contract—you get the point. I like this practice not only because it gives me the warm fuzzies, but also because it helps me identify values or actions that I can put into practice now and in the short-term while I work my way towards a one-day dream future.[5]

I'd like you to describe your ideal experiences for your goals, habits, focus, and boundaries in Exercise 3. There are three rules for this exercise: be honest, be realistic, and be specific.

Be honest and check in with yourself as you're writing—are you listing things you feel like you "should" do, or are you writing down what you truly desire? It can be challenging to differentiate the feeling of desire versus doing something out of obligation to follow the rules. Consider, for example, how you feel in your mind and body when you are curious and satisfied—the feeling should not be attached to resentment or overwhelm. Try to identify the difference between doing something that makes you feel proud and confident and doing something you feel like you "just have to do" because it would impress someone else.

Be realistic about what is actually feasible for you. The goal is to set yourself up for success, not set yourself up for potential negative self-talk if you don't hit a goal. For example, I have chronic back pain that is exacerbated from sitting, so I would not write "I'd like to work for 6 hours every weekend at my favorite coffee shop" because I know that while I love the café's lo-fi jams playlist and matcha oat milk lattes, sitting that long on a wooden bench would cause me physical pain. A more realistic idea would be an open-ended "work at the coffee shop on the weekends," leaving space for adapting to what my body needs at the moment.[6]

Be specific and write not only what you'd like to create or do or make, but also how you'd like to feel during the process. How would your body, mind, and spirit feel? For example, would you feel calm? Energized? Curious? Relaxed? Unrushed? Focused?

Exercise 3:
My Ideal Relationship with My Habits, Goals, Focus, and Boundaries

To complete this exercise, answer the following questions about your relationship with your productivity practices in your notebook or document. Include examples as evidence, and feel free to replace the word "relationship" with "experience" if that feels more concrete to you.

- My ideal relationship with my habits would be...
- My ideal relationship with my goals would be...
- My ideal relationship with focus would be...
- My ideal relationship with setting boundaries around my work/technology use/etc. would be...

Great work brainstorming so far! I hope that you're beginning to view your personal productivity practice through a lens of curiosity. Your next activity will be determining a specific project or goal that you'd like to accomplish with the help of this book so that you have a practical way to apply the activities in each chapter. Chapter 2, "Setting Goals You Can Reach," will teach you how to set actionable and achievable goals, but I have faith that you can identify a preliminary goal or project here in the introduction. Please note that I will use the words "goal" and "project" interchangeably throughout this book when I refer to the larger accomplishment you are attempting to complete.

Here are some examples of projects or goals this book could help you accomplish: build a website, start a business, write a dissertation, write a book, write a term paper, develop lesson plans for a course you want to teach, declutter your house, create choreography for a show, learn to draw comics, complete a self-directed or asynchronous course, teach yourself how to sew your own clothes, develop a yoga or running practice, learn to cook a particular meal, etc.

You'll notice that these sample goals and projects range in the length of time they require for completion, the types of labor they call for (mental, physical, emotional, or a combination of the three), and in the level of embedded accountability. I share them all in one fell swoop to show you that productivity does not apply only to tasks in the academic and business world. Remember, productivity actually means accomplishing the tasks you set out to complete, no matter your goals. Feel free to get creative!

Exercise 4:
Identifying My Goal

So, what goal would you like to attempt in this go-around with *Tend to It*? If you're unsure which goal you want to focus on, try writing a list of all the things you would *like* to accomplish in the next month, quarter, or year. Try not to get caught up in worrying, "How will I ever do these things?," because the purpose here is to brainstorm.

To complete this exercise, write five to 10 potential goals in your notebook or document. Then, look back through your list and choose just one to focus on for the purpose of working through *Tend to It*. Highlight it or circle it, so you know it's "the one."

Chapter 1:
Habits Can Be Our Friends

H abit formation was one of the first topics that fascinated me on my personal productivity path. I was drawn to study and practice habits because they promised me the magic of checking something off my to-do list without needing to harness massive willpower.

A Quick Note on Spoon Theory

Habits are essential to me because being chronically ill means I need to manage the effort I expend on different activities. Like some other chronically ill people, I use Spoon Theory to communicate how much effort or energy—also called "spoons"—I have to expend on accomplishing tasks like self-care, work, and hobbies. By allocating a limited number of metaphorical spoons to "spend" on each activity, I intend to preserve spoons throughout the day.[7] Spoon Theory is subjective, so I may start a day with 20 spoons and another day with five; similarly, if I am having a chronic illness or pain flare, it may take three spoons to do a "simple" task like showering, whereas showering on a non-flare day requires a single spoon's worth of energy. While it is not always possible to preserve my spoons, I find that habits can help me limit expending spoons on decision-making. If you also experience chronic health issues that affect your energy levels or ability to focus, you may be interested in using Spoon Theory to navigate your own productivity practices.

What are Habits?

Behaviors become habits when we no longer have to rely upon our willpower to do them. **When I say willpower, I am referring to our determination to complete a particular action or task.** According to *Psychology Today*, "the behavioral patterns we repeat most often are literally etched into our neural pathways," which results in behaviors becoming automatic.[8] Habits researcher Gretchen Rubin's *Better Than Before* is focused on habit formation. She writes in the "about" page for her book: "Habits are the invisible architecture of daily life. We repeat about 40% of our behavior almost daily, so if we change our habits, we change our lives."[9]

The action of performing a habit can be broken down into a formula:

Cue → Routine → Reward

If you say you want to begin or stop a habit, you are likely thinking about the *routine*. However, to change a routine, you need to be conscious of what *cues* you to act and what *rewards* you receive for doing your routine action. Cues can be certain times of the day, emotions, sounds, smells, feelings, sights, or other stimuli that prompt you to action. Rewards can range from a tasty treat to human connection to personal satisfaction to avoiding conflict to something else entirely, depending on what feels rewarding to you as an individual. To build a new habit, I often create a cue by writing myself a note and hanging it on the wall or the mirror where I'll see it, or I set a pop-up reminder on my phone or laptop to remind me to do a particular action at a particular time. Sometimes I will write the reward in the reminder to motivate me, just in case I feel like skipping out on the new routine.

A common habit to show the cue → routine → reward formula in action is procrastination. We procrastinate when we want to avoid doing a task we don't want to do. Some popular procrastination routines include cleaning out our email inboxes or our fridges, scrolling social media on our phones, or texting a friend to strike up a conversation.

When we do these alternative routines instead of the task we originally intended to accomplish, we receive a reward, which may be the dopamine hit of seeing a new heart on a social media post, feeling accomplished for cleaning, or laughing with a friend.

Here is a visual breakdown of procrastination into the cue → routine → reward formula:

- Cue: You open up a report you've been working on, and you begin to feel bored within the first five minutes of writing.

- Routine: Before you know you're doing it, you've opened up a web browser and are checking your social media account.

- Reward: You feel immediate satisfaction when you see that people have liked your recent post.

As you can see in this example, the immediate satisfaction of seeing a heart or thumbs up on social media is a reward for the habit of procrastinating on a work task. Here's another breakdown of how procrastination works:

- Cue: You open up the report you've been working on, and begin to feel bored.

- Routine: When you feel the urge to check social media, you activate your internet blocker app and take a short break to make a cup of your favorite coffee.

- Reward: You get to enjoy a delicious drink while you write your report.

I used procrastination as an example of a habit to show you that two identical cues—feeling bored—can trigger different routines. To replace the routine of procrastination with the routine of finishing your intended tasks, you need to consciously consider the reward. Here is another example that uses morning routines.

Morning Routine 1:

- Cue: Your alarm clock goes off.
- Routine: You snooze the alarm for half an hour.
- Reward: You get to stay cozy and warm and sleep a little more.

Morning Routine 2:

- Cue: Your alarm clock goes off.
- Routine: You allow yourself to hit snooze *only once* and then wake up.
- Reward: You have time to make coffee and stretch before you start your day.

Without valuing either the sleeping in or waking up earlier option as "better" or "worse," I want to note the impact that the reward has on the routine. If you wanted to establish a habit to wake up earlier, you could motivate yourself with how nice it feels to drink your coffee without rushing and with the knowledge that stretching before you start your day helps to keep pain levels down throughout the day.

It's time to practice breaking down a couple of your habits into the cue → routine → reward formula. Exercise 5 aims to get you to see your actions through a lens of intention and self-awareness. You don't have to actually change any of your habits now—just practice identifying cues, routines, and rewards.

Exercise 5:
Breaking Down My Habits into Cues, Routines, and Rewards

This exercise will ask you to break down two habits into the cue → routine → reward formula. First, identify one of your current habits and write it in your notebook or document. Then, describe what *cues you to act* on that habit, what *actions you take* during your routine, and what *reward motivates* you to act as you do. Then repeat the same activity for a second habit. You can use the examples from above about procrastination and sleeping in as a model.

Once you've broken down two habits into the cue → routine → reward formula, examine both lists and journal your answers to the following questions. Are there any similarities between your cues, routines, or rewards? Are there any differences? What does breaking down your habits show you about your motivations, preferences, or priorities?

This chapter offered you an introduction to habit formation. I included it at the beginning because the tools and practices that follow—setting goals, focusing, and establishing boundaries around your work and your technology use—can all become habits. When we recognize that our routines are prompted by cues and tied to rewards, we can make decisions with more intention and awareness. If you want to do a deeper dive into habit formation through an exercise that breaks down the cue → routine → reward process even further, I recommend you read my e-zine, "To Hold in The Hand: A Guide to Maintaining," which you can access via thetendingyear.com/newsletter.

Chapter 2:
Setting Goals You Can Reach

I've always been good at school, from the time I was spelling words like "encyclopedia" in first grade through completing my graduate degrees. I loved school for three reasons: 1) I received praise for doing well at something I enjoyed (learning), 2) I usually had an explicit goal to achieve, and 3) I knew what criteria were required to do well on each goal. For example, in graduate school, I knew that a term paper needed to be 20 pages and include 10 sources, or I knew that my comprehensive exam defense was two hours long and I would be expected to know 60 sources well enough to answer questions about them. I even broke my dissertation chapters down into components and checklists. All that being said, merely having a tidy checklist won't stop the onslaught of overlapping deadlines or magically teach you how to prioritize. When you feel overwhelmed with options and boxes to check off, it is time to look to your goals for guidance on how to proceed.

When I finished my PhD, I decided to focus on developing my business as a writer and coach instead of pursuing the tenure track as a professor. However, my key goals are still educating myself and others. The difference between my pursuit of knowledge now versus my experience in academia is that I now determine my *own* goals, set my *own* deadlines, and hold *myself* accountable for meeting them. When I set a goal I'd like to accomplish, my next step is to identify what I need to do, when I need to do it, and what satisfactory outcomes should look like. I set myself up to thrive when I make my goals *actionable* and *achievable*, two terms that I'll define for you later in this chapter.

Before we get into setting goals, let's make sure we are all on the same page about what "goals" actually are. **A goal is a desired result that you hope to achieve. It's the endpoint of your labors: the accomplishment made tangible.** A goal is different from an intention, which is how you plan to get to the place you want to get to. I know that may sound trippy, so let me share examples.

- If your *goal* is to get a good participation grade in your class, you may set an *intention* to read the course material and highlight sections you can talk about during the class discussion.

- If your *goal* is to be a better friend, you may set an *intention* to practice active listening.

- If your *goal* is to learn how to do a headstand in yoga, you may set an *intention* to approach your practice with lighthearted humor and acceptance when you sometimes fall down.

- If your *goal* is to increase the blank space in your day, you may set an *intention* to say "let me get back to you" and take some time to check in with yourself before you accept invites from others.

Starting to make sense? The goal is where you want to get to one day, and setting an intention can help you make small daily choices that will help you work your way to the cumulative, more significant goal.[10]

Let's Set Some Goals

It's time to start working with goals! Look back to Exercise 4, where you identified the goal you'd like to work on this time around with *Tend to It*. Now that we've differentiated goals from intentions, take some time to modify your goal if you need to. If you revise your goal, be sure to write it down so you remember! I'm going to use "publishing an article in a magazine" as my sample goal throughout this chapter, so I'll do the exercises along with you as a model.

The Actionable and Achievable Goals System

The words "actionable" and "achievable" are similar in that they both refer to something you can accomplish. However, I use them in different ways to guide how I plan, work, and track my progress from start to finish. Before I get into the "how" of actionable and achievable goals, allow me to explain what the approaches are.

Actionable

An actionable goal has explicit steps. To set (and follow through on!) an actionable goal, you should identify the precise steps you will need to take, from beginning to end. Each step should be broken down into its smallest component tasks, and it's crucial here that you identify exact actions to take—versus general actions on a to-do list, such as "write a chapter" or "learn Spanish." For example, to write a chapter, you'd need to choose a topic, a thesis, and sources to analyze, write a first draft, revise, etc. To learn Spanish, you'd need to select a teacher, program, or application, learn the alphabet and parts of speech, etc. I'll break down an example goal a few pages later in this book.

Achievable

An achievable goal is one that you can accomplish given your skills, timeline, access, and motivation. Goals are not automatically achievable; we need to adjust our approach to make them so. For example, while a professional pastry chef may easily whip up a gluten-free birthday cake in two hours, the same task would not be equally achievable to someone who does not share the same training, timeline, and access to materials. Approaching our goals with an awareness of what can make the tasks more achievable for us as individuals is key.

Make Your Goal Actionable: Identify "Done"

To make your goal actionable, you should begin by identifying a "done" point that feels satisfactory for your purposes. By identifying what satisfactory completion of your goal looks like now, you will be able to reverse engineer your process from start to finish. You may also be able to streamline your focus and finish your goal more quickly (I'm thinking here of the phrase that gets thrown around in academia: "A good dissertation is a done dissertation").

Here's my answer to the question "What will 'done' look like for this goal?" using my example goal of publishing an article in a magazine: I will have pitched, drafted, and revised an article that is accepted for publication, and I will have a scheduled date when my article will be published. Complete this practice for your own goal in Exercise 6.

Exercise 6:
What Will "Done" Look Like for My Goal?

In your notebook or document, describe what completion of your goal will look like. **Instead of aiming for perfection (which may delay your completion of the goal), identify a "done" that feels good enough to complete the project successfully and move on.** Another way to view this question is, "How will I know that I'm done?" or "What will my final project look like?"

Make Your Goal Actionable: Break It Down

Once you have identified what a satisfactory "done" would look like for your goal, your next step should be writing down EVERY action you will need to take to accomplish your goal, from start to finish. It's essential that you do not skip over any steps, even if they seem insignificant or too small to write down.

Here is why I want you to do this. When we set goals that are too broad, like "write a book," we have to wrack our brains to choose which specific tasks we should do when we actually start working. If you already have an exact list of tasks to accomplish and you know in which order you should complete them, you will be able to focus your energy on achieving specific, tangible activities during your work sessions. Not only this, but you will complete the tasks in a way that scaffolds your progress. To-do lists are motivational because we feel satisfied when we check things off, so consider the exact steps you write in your Exercise 7 plan to be your to-do list.

Here is my answer to the question "What are all the steps involved?" using my example of publishing an article in a magazine.

- Review a few of the magazines I may want to pitch to.
- Choose which magazine to pitch to.
- Look up the magazine's submission policies.
- If they're currently accepting what I want to pitch, draft up a pitch or two.
- Get feedback from a friend about my pitch.
- Revise my pitch as needed.
- Submit my pitch to the editor.
- If the pitch isn't accepted, don't give up hope! Revise and resubmit it to the same or another magazine.
- When the pitch is accepted, celebrate!

- Talk about the article with a friend to bounce ideas.
- Outline my article.
- Write my first article draft.
- Get feedback from a friend on the first draft.
- Revise the article into my second draft.
- Repeat the previous two steps as many times as needed.
- Submit my revised draft to the magazine.
- Revise per the magazine editor's suggestions.
- Have a friend proofread my edits.
- Revise again as needed, per friend's suggestions.
- Repeat the previous two steps as many times as needed.
- Do a final proofread.
- Draft bio for the magazine, if needed.
- Source author photo for the magazine, if needed.
- Submit article and any additional materials.
- Confirm publication date.
- Celebrate!

As you can see, I broke my process down into very small steps, in order, and I was sure to include revision and celebration on my list.

Exercise 7:
What Steps Do I Need to Take in Order to Complete My Goal?

Now it's your turn! Write your list of every step you need to take in your notebook or document. If you aren't sure what some of the steps are for completing your goal, put "research steps involved" at the top of your list and then go spend some time researching and check that task off the list! You can ask a friend or mentor who has completed a similar goal before, do online research, or brainstorm potential tasks and write them down as fillers for now.

It's totally okay if you end up adding, reordering, or cutting out tasks as you progress further on your goal. The most important thing at the beginning is breaking down the larger goal into small tasks—and don't forget to include rest, recovery, and celebration on your list. Take your time with this exercise, using as many pages as necessary.

Make Your Goal Achievable

The benchmark of "achievable" will look different for everyone, depending on the project's context and on your individual strengths, preferences, accessibility needs, training, emotional capacity, and financial access. However, when we consider the achievability of a task, we should also consider our conceptualization of "success" as it relates to perfectionism and obsessions with work.

The way we perceive achievement has been influenced by systems of oppression under capitalism, which goes hand in hand with white supremacy. White supremacy is perpetuated through actions such as obsessions with gaining and hoarding wealth, the normalization of perfectionism and workaholism, and the systemic inaccessibility of resources like housing, healthcare, food and clean water, and legal protections. Additionally, white supremacy under capitalism attributes success to an individual's "hard work" while ignoring systems of oppression. As a result, the systemic disempowering of underrepresented groups is a method of gaslighting people for "not trying hard enough."

When people feel that they "should" be able to do certain productive tasks, they may turn to self-shame if they cannot achieve those tasks; similarly, when people feel like their worth is tied to their work, they may disdain others who work differently than they do within systems of oppression under capitalism. I hope that personalizing the goal setting practice will help people resist normalizing an obsession with a standardized, perfectionistic vision of "success." For example, by checking in with what feels loving and empowering and ethical to you, you may choose to say "no" to traditional white supremacist categories of success, such as relying on a top-down hierarchy of decision-making that ignores voices of critique. I also want to acknowledge that a white supremacist obsession with overwork under a system of capitalism harms BIPOC in different ways than it harms white people. When practicing personal productivity within a culture of deep-seated racism (particularly concerning work that has been mandated, underpaid, and undervalued), BIPOC may additionally rely on tactics created by BIPOC for BIPOC that incorporate radical rest practices, such as those published by Tricia Hersey, Rachel Cargle, and Sonya Renee Taylor. Finally, white people should make choices around how they discuss productivity with a critical awareness of their own complicity in perpetuating standards of success based on exclusion.[11]

While each person's definition of "achievable" will fluctuate, I encourage everyone to start by answering the following questions. The purpose of these questions is to help you feel motivated and in control of your process by individualizing the process. Let's begin with your "why."[12]

Exercise 8:
What is Your "Why" or Purpose for Accomplishing Your Goal?

The first question I would like you to answer is why you want to accomplish this goal. Another way to ask this is, "What is my 'why' or purpose for accomplishing my goal?" You may have one or multiple answers. My "why" for publishing articles in magazines is to make my research accessible to more readers, introduce myself to people as an expert in my field, and make connections with editors and publishers.

Brainstorm your "why" or purpose in your notebook or document, then write down a concise phase or word for your "why" or purpose and display it in your workspace as a consistent reminder and motivator. Bonus points for making the sign aesthetically pleasing, as this may make you feel cheery and excited!

Make Your Goal Achievable: Use Accountability to Your Benefit

My next question for you is about what types of accountability will enable you to do your best at your goal. Accountability doesn't need to be a deadline set by a boss (although it could be)—**accountability is any plan you make ahead of time that will enable you to show up, do the work, and complete the tasks you set out to complete**. For my magazine example, my accountability includes determining deadlines with my friends and any editors who will be reading my drafts, setting word counts I want to hit, and scheduling co-working sessions with friends and colleagues when I'll do my writing and revising. It's also important to hold yourself accountable with joyful rewards, like creating or reading for pleasure. Sleep and basic self-care should *not* be considered a "reward"—they are necessary requirements for living a healthy life!

Exercise 9:
What Kinds of Accountability Will Make My Process More Enjoyable & Achievable?

Brainstorm ways that you can use accountability to help you accomplish the tasks you listed in Exercise 7. Write your answers to the following questions in your notebook or document.

What types of accountability will be helpful for particular tasks, times, or stages of your process?

Will you need more accountability at the beginning, middle, and/or end of your process?

What are some joyful rewards you will celebrate with?

Make Your Goal Achievable: Be Aware of the Planning Fallacy

So far, you have identified a goal, named what a satisfactory "done" would look like, broken down the process into specific steps, honed in on what is motivating you to accomplish your goal, and brainstormed how to include accountability in your approach. Now it's time to learn about the Planning Fallacy.

The Planning Fallacy occurs when we underestimate the amount of labor and time required to complete a task. We do this because we feel optimistic and biased that we can complete a task in a short time frame. This could be because we forget to factor in how long it will take us to complete non-project related tasks (i.e., cooking, commuting, cleaning, resting, etc.). Additionally, we can become so confident that we forget that history proves we need longer time-frames to complete similar tasks.

Here's an example of the Planning Fallacy in action: when I started my comprehensive exams in my graduate program, I told my friends, "I'll have this done in a few weeks." All I had to do was read 60 texts and write two 15-page papers. I was used to writing 15-page final papers over a weekend, and I had regularly read 10 texts in a week for graduate classes. How different could reading for my comprehensive exams be? The answer: a freaking lot. I ended up spending about a year researching, writing, revising my papers, and preparing for my defense.

I used to do this with work all the time, too. I chose arbitrary deadlines to impress my boss ("I'll get this to you by the end of the day") and then scrambled to meet them or backtracked and asked for an extension—neither of which felt good. I could easily have said, "I'll have this to you in three days" and received a genuine "sounds great!" Instead, I set *way* too early of a deadline because I wanted that timeline to be true. Remaining aware of the Planning Fallacy helps us wait a beat and check in with reality before setting a deadline that will unnecessarily overtax us.

Exercise 10:
Make it Achievable with Ease and Time

Look back at your list of steps for your goals (Exercise 7). Each one of these steps should be an individual task, so take some time to break the steps down into sub-tasks if necessary. Then, answer the following questions in your notebook or document. The purpose here is to gain greater awareness and confidence about the length of time and level of commitment each task will require.

- Which tasks will be the quickest to accomplish?
- Which tasks will be the easiest to accomplish with my current skill set?
- Which tasks will take the longest to complete?
- Which tasks will be the most complicated or require the most focus, critical thinking, physical/mental/emotional energy, etc.?

Feel free to rank any of your answers if that is helpful for you: quickest to longest, easiest to hardest, least to most complicated, etc.

Now that you know which tasks will be easiest, hardest, quickest, and longest, write down some plans for how you want to approach the different tasks. For example, do you want to save the easy tasks for when you want a quick win? Do you want to schedule the complicated tasks for early in the day? Do you want to work on your long tasks a little each week for a month? Use your notebook or document to brainstorm approaches that will compassionately set future you up for success.

Prioritize Rest

The final activity for setting a goal is identifying how you will rest and recharge as you progress towards its completion. When we make rest and recharge plans, we should acknowledge that we often expend personal resources like energy, focus, or spoons beyond our work sessions on tasks that are required to care for ourselves and our loved ones, like cooking, cleaning, grocery shopping, etc. Therefore, if possible, I encourage you to allocate time and space to rest and recharge outside of your many professional and personal labors.

Exercise 11:
Make a Rest and Recharge Plan

Use your notebook or document to brainstorm what you want resting and recharging to look and feel like as you progress on your goal. When will you rest? How will you restore yourself? Get creative! If you feel stuck, check out the list of rest and recharge activities in my blog post "Make a Rest and Recharge Toolkit" at www.thetendingyear.com/2-16-make-a-rest-and-recharge-toolkit/.

I hope that this chapter has provided you with a greater understanding of setting goals, breaking down projects into actionable tasks, and making achievable plans to complete the requisite tasks. The activities we practiced were:

- Identifying a goal as different from an intention.

- Identifying what "done" looks like for your goal.

- Breaking the goal down into individual tasks and sub-tasks.

- Naming your "why" or your purpose for accomplishing this goal.

- Discerning what external accountability can help you complete your goal.

- Determining the varying levels of ease and time required to complete particular tasks.

- Identifying methods for completing individual tasks without falling prey to the Planning Fallacy.

- Imagining how to prioritize resting and recharging as you progress on your goal.

Take some time to complete these exercises and activities before you move on to Chapter 3, "How to Focus with Intention," which will teach you what to do during work sessions.

Chapter 3:
How to Focus with Intention

When I developed chronic health issues in 2017, my ability to focus went downhill. I was often in pain and I felt disheartened when I sat down at my desk to work. I felt so overwhelmed with the number of tasks on my to-do list that I frantically bounced from activity to activity, never truly completing anything. Other times, I would force myself to work way past my comfort level, deep into the evening, to complete an individual task to perfection as a fleeting attempt at gaining control over my life.

Thankfully, I acknowledged my workaholic tendencies and learned how to use tools that enabled me to limit the time I spent working by helping me focus on individual activities without distraction. This chapter will teach you how to use the focus tools that my coaching clients and I have found to be the most helpful. Specifically, I'll cover how to stop procrastinating on aversive tasks, how to "batchotask" (a practice I created that blends batching and mono-tasking), and how to use pulse and pause methods to limit distractions, stay motivated, and prioritize taking breaks.

How to Handle an Aversive Task

There are as many reasons for struggling with focus as there are for struggling to accomplish goals. However, a few critical focus road-blocks include getting distracted, trying to do too many things at once, not being clear about what we're trying to accomplish, and procrastinating to avoid aversive tasks.

Aversive tasks are things that we need to do but that we avoid doing because they make us feel or think about things we don't enjoy. They're the opposite of "fun." Procrastination researcher Timothy Pychyl identified six different attributes of aversive tasks: boring, frustrating, difficult, unstructured or ambiguous, lacking personal meaning, and lacking intrinsic rewards.[13] If we resent the idea of doing a task because we think the experience will prove challenging or uncomfortable, we are more likely to say, "I'll just do it later" and revert to procrastination. In order to change your procrastination habits, you need to address your aversive tasks and create an action plan for addressing why the tasks feel aversive to you. Continue to Exercise 12 to do a four-step exercise that will guide you through making an action plan to finally check your aversive tasks off your to-do list.

Exercise 12:
Three Steps to Handle Aversive Tasks

Step 1: Recognize That You're Dealing with an Aversive Task

Your first step is to notice when you're procrastinating and check in on why you don't want to do the task you should be doing. In your notebook or document, write a list of three to five aversive tasks that you've been procrastinating on accomplishing. If you're writing in a notebook, leave some space under each task so you can fill in answers to Step 2 and Step 3. Once you have your list of aversive tasks, use Pychyl's list of six attributes of aversive tasks (boring, frustrating, difficult, unstructured or ambiguous, lacking in personal meaning, and lacking in intrinsic rewards) and feel free to add your own to identify why you have been avoiding doing the task. Write the attribute (boring, difficult, etc.) next to the task.

Step 2: Make A Plan of Attack (or A Plan of Attempt)

Once you have identified what makes the task so aversive to you, it's time to get creative about establishing a new approach to the task. Productivity researcher Nils Salzgeber suggests in his article "To Procrastinate Less, Make Tasks More Attractive" that we can make aversive tasks more appealing by doing four actions:

- Connecting tasks to your values and future goals
- Gamifying the task
- Promising yourself a reward
- Pairing the task with something tempting (treat, music, etc.)

We can use methods like these to increase our intrigue for aversive tasks. Look over the list you wrote in Step 1 and imagine how you can use strategies to make the task more appealing. If you feel stuck, here are some ideas: Can you find motivation by equating completing this task with getting one step closer to a future dream (values and goals)? Can you see how much you can accomplish in two hours (game)? Can you promise to stop working for the day when you finish the task (reward)? Can you drink a fancy coffee while you work (pairing)? Write the potential method next to your tasks.

Step 3: Find Out the Best Way to Just Do the Damn Thing

Once you've identified why the task feels aversive and you've imagined how you can flip its yuck into a yum (or at least into an "okay, this is fine, I can do this"), your next step is to finalize a practical approach. Maybe Step 2 convinced you to dive into the work, but if you are still struggling to jumpstart your labor, try answering some of the following questions, which will give you a specific map for doing the task.

- Where will I do this task?
- When will I do it?
- How long will I spend on it?
- Is it better to do it in steps or to do it all at once?
- Do I need to ask for help doing it?
- Do I want someone to look over my work once I'm done?
- Do I need accountability (i.e., working alongside others)?
- Is there a way to make doing it more comfortable?
- How will I feel when the task is accomplished?

Use your answers to construct an effective plan for your work session.

"Batchotasking" Part One: Batching

The word "batch" is both a noun and a verb. You may have heard the noun form of it in terms of whipping up a batch of cookies. (One of the definitions for batch is literally "the quantity baked at one time."[14]) Slap on a gerund, and you get a verb form: batching.

When we apply this term to productivity, batching means assigning a particular task to a specific day and time—and then giving ourselves permission to *only* work on that task during that day and time. Batching is a popular method among entrepreneurs, who may, for example, dedicate Monday to one task, such as recording podcasts, Tuesday to another, such as working with clients, Wednesday to another, such as writing content, etc. But anyone can batch their professional and personal tasks.

Batching can help you to:

- Practice setting healthy boundaries around work, since it requires you to put tasks back on the shelf when you end your batching time. (This is particularly important for people with workaholic tendencies.)
- Identify which goals are truly achievable for a particular batching session.
- Prioritize your highest impact tasks for days and times when you may have more energy and the ability to focus.
- Make habit formation easier because you can tie particular cues and rewards to batched routines.

"Batchotasking" Part Two: Monotasking

When we think we are multitasking, we are actually *task switching*. I like the way productivity researcher Chris Bailey describes the discrepancy between the two practices: "It's impossible for our brains to focus on two tasks at once—it's actually rapidly switching between them. Instead of channeling our complete focus and energy into one task, we spread it thin, which prevents us from diving deep into any one of our tasks."[15] In other words, when we think we are multitasking, we are repeatedly pulling our focus away from not only one task, but two of them!

If task switching actually makes us perform worse at our tasks, why would we do it? Remember when I talked about the hits of dopamine we feel when we procrastinate? When we quickly switch between tasks, we feel as if we are crossing multiple things off our to-do list, which releases dopamine into our systems. When we try to multitask/task switch instead of deeply focusing on just one task for an extended period, we often end up overwhelmed, confused as to why we haven't been more successful, and we judge ourselves for not being further along.

How to Set Yourself Up for "Batchotask" Success

To "batchotask," all you have to do is batch your monotasking into sessions.

You might be concerned, wondering, "That is too much structure for me. I'm a rhythm person and don't like to be tied down to a predetermined to-do list. I like to go with the flow and see where my interests take me." Don't worry: "batchotasking" works with routines, rhythms, depth, breadth, inspiration, brainstorming, stream of consciousness creation, and other preferences. The only requirement is that you focus on one general task in one general time…and don't task switch!

To "batchotask" successfully, I encourage you to develop a plan ahead of time. To do this, you will need to select a task and select a time. You can make this as general or as specific as you prefer.

Here's an example:

General	Specific
Wednesday: Work on my dissertation chapter in the morning. *Activity*: Read or write with an end goal of writing 10,000 words by the end of the month.	*Wednesday*: Morning dissertation routine. *Activity*: 7-8 am: Stretch, breakfast, coffee/water; 8-11am: Work at home, do 3 tasks: 1) Set 3 dissertation goals and write them in my dissertation journal before I work (one should be to write 333 words, others can include reading and taking notes), 2) Use pulse and pause method to be sure to take breaks (move my body on breaks—no screens!) 3) Use my final work session to record daily dissertation progress in my dissertation journal.

Both lists say the same thing: work on that dissertation! While some people may prefer the freedom of the "General" side, I personally prefer working with a predetermined checklist. In fact, this "Specific" list was literally my exact morning routine for some time when I was writing my dissertation.

How to Stay on "Batchotask"

Avoid e-distractions. Worried about the endless distractions of social media or online shopping or Googling "photos of baby animals"? Try an internet blocker. You can see a list of cheap and free internet and selective website blockers in the recommended resources at the end of this book.

Stick a fork in it. When you finish your "batchotasking" session, put that task back on the shelf for the day or the week. If you mono-tasked, focused, and tried your best, then you've done everything you can, and thus you did an excellent job! Give yourself permission to leave that task within its "batchotasked" boundaries, check it off your to-do list, and move on to your other batched monotasks...which includes things like hanging with friends without checking work email on your phone! Remember: you can "batchotask" any activity by scheduling it into its own time. If you struggle to make time to play or rest, "batchotask" it into your calendar.

Use a pulse and pause method. This method will help you focus during work sessions and ensure that you take breaks. I'll introduce this method soon, but first, I'd like you to complete Exercise 13.

Exercise 13:
Make a "Batchotasking" Plan

Look at your list of tasks from Exercise 7 and identify a task that you can "batchotask." Then, look at your calendar and set aside a block of time when you'll work *only* on *that task*. Block that time off in your calendar right now.

Once you've chosen your task and your time, write a General and/or Specific "batchotasking plan" in your notebook or computer document, using the previous General and Specific lists as a model. You can get as detailed as you want to (or not), but be sure to limit your list to one task and to one day or time of day.

You can schedule multiple "batchotasked" tasks or projects in one day—just be sure that you don't overlap tasks and you give yourself a break between activities!

One of My Favorite Tools: The Pulse and Pause Method

The pulse and pause method is incredible. The process itself is quite simple: you work without distraction on a task for a predetermined amount of time (pulse), and then you take a break (pause). I'll break the process down further below so you can learn how to get the most out of each step.

Out of all of the coaching sessions I've had, my clients have found the most success with the pulse and pause method, and I credit it as one of the five productivity practices that helped me finish my dissertation.[16] The method has four steps: choose what to do, set a timer and work, take a break, and repeat.

How to Use the Pulse and Pause Method

Step 1: Choose Your Work Time and Choose What to Do

The first step in the pulse and pause method is determining how long you'd like to "pulse" or work for. Some popular options are 25 minutes, 45 minutes, or 90 minutes, but you should choose a set time that works well for you. Feel free to experiment to find your optimal pulse session, and also feel free to switch it up as needed.

Next, identify a task you could accomplish in your pulse timeframe. It is important that you choose an actionable and achievable goal for your work session. Lucky for you, you already have a list of goals to choose from—your list of steps from Exercise 7. If you're pulling a task from your list, you may not be able to fully complete the entire task in a shorter pulse session, so you can set a goal to do a portion of the task. In other words, your pulse session goal might be "begin to do ___" or "complete first third of ____." Here's a tip: time how long it takes you to finish specific tasks so you can have a rough estimate of how many "pulses" you will need to spend on them.

Step 2: Set a Timer and Work

Set your timer for the timeframe you decided and start working. You can use a clock, kitchen timer, or free application like BeFocused[17], Forest[18], or website like tomato-timer.com/. You can see a list of more timers in the recommended resources at the end of this book.

Say NO to distractions while you work: do not check your email, do not check your text messages, and, if possible, ask people around you not to interrupt you during your predetermined pulse session. You can even put your phone on "do not disturb" mode or write yourself a sticky note and put it on your phone or laptop that says "stay focused for X minutes!"

Step 3: Take a Break

When the timer goes off after your pulse session, set another timer for a predetermined amount of time and take a break. If possible, stretch your body, look away from your screen, or go get a drink of water. It's popular to take a five minute pause between pulse sessions, but you can take ten, fifteen, or more minutes depending on what works best for you.

Step 4: Repeat Steps 1, 2, and 3 and Then Take a Longer Break

Choose another actionable and achievable task for your next pulse session. This might mean picking up where you left off or starting a new task. Up to you! Set a timer and do focused work for your prede-termined pulse session time, then take another short break, repeating that process. Some people like to do two or four pulse sessions before they take a longer break.

Remember that you can choose how long you want to spend working and taking breaks. You should predetermine your pulse or work sessions as well as your pause or break sessions so you know when to start and stop working. Maybe you only have an hour to work, so you do two pulse sessions of 20 minutes each with two ten-minute breaks; perhaps you want to work for ten minutes or ninety minutes at a time. There's no "better" way to do it, just as long as you 1) identify a task to accomplish during your work session, 2) work without distractions, and 3) take breaks.

Some Final Focus Activities

Now that you've learned some tools that can enhance your focus, let's close this chapter by making an informed focus plan. The next two exercises will help you to identify potential obstacles ahead of time and imagine multiple ways to navigate any roadblocks that may pop up while you're focusing. They are multistep exercises, so please take your time with them.

Exercise 14:
Look for Patterns in Distraction and Aversion

First, write a list in your notebook or document of common distractions you encounter when you're trying to focus.

Next, identify and list some aversive tasks that you've been putting off. These could be tasks you've mentioned in previous exercises, but they don't have to be.

Finally, review your common distractions and aversive task lists and look for patterns and similarities. Record any overlaps you notice about your behavior. What new information does this provide for you?

Exercise 15:
Make an Informed Focus Plan

Choose a task from your list for Exercise 7. Then, using the awareness you gained in Exercise 14, create a focus plan by answering the following questions in your notebook or document.

- What task would I like to work on?
- What steps will I need to take to complete it?
- When will I work on this task (batching)?
- What distractions will I be up against (monotasking)?
- What actions should I take to help me avoid these distractions?
- How will I make sure that I stay focused during my work sessions?

For the Pulse and Pause Method

- What will I do during my short breaks between pulse sessions?
- What will I do during my long breaks between pulse and pause sessions?

Chapter 4:
Gain Clarity and Set Boundaries

As someone who spent 10 years in three graduate programs, I was steeped in the workaholic culture of graduate school and academia at large.[19] If you go back and read *The Tending Year* across the two years when I was blogging every week during my doctoral studies, you can trace my growing fascination with setting boundaries around work. For example, I was amazed to learn that stopping to take breaks was actually MORE productive than forcing myself to work out of workaholic shame.

Many of the practices and tools that helped me set boundaries around my work are covered in this book. Yet, one of my most significant changes was giving myself permission to set boundaries around my own relationship with work. This was much easier to do once I learned the approaches that I'll cover in this chapter, such as Parkinson's Law, which resulted in one of my favorite creations, the Goldilocks Approach to Productivity.

This chapter is all about gaining clarity and setting boundaries around your work and your output, including your technology use. My hope is that you will compassionately evaluate your own relationship with your work. I also hope that the tools I teach you will enable you to set boundaries with yourself, with your colleagues and bosses, and that together we can push back against the "always-on" culture of workaholism. However, in our efforts to reimagine productivity culture, we must be careful not to perpetuate a perspective that setting self-reflexive boundaries around work is a sign of "morality" or a mark of "success." Indeed, there are many ways to work, and some people who work in a labor force, who may or may not be academics and creatives, may not as easily have access to set the boundaries I suggest—nor may they find them applicable. There is a larger conversation to be had here, and I hope to continue participating in it. For now, I ask that you please take what works for you from this chapter, tweak it to your particular experience, and do not feel as if you must apply my suggestions to be "good" or "successful" with productivity.

Check Yourself with Parkinson's Law

When I learned about Parkinson's Law, fireworks went off in my brain. This concept, introduced by Cyril Northcote Parkinson in a 1955 article in *The Economist*, states that work will expand to fill the time we allow for its completion. Because I understand things better when I use visual metaphors, I like to perceive this as "work will expand to fill the size of the vessel we provide for it." For example, if you have a task to complete and you give yourself a whole week to do it, you will likely take the entire week to dawdle on the task and complete it near the end, anyways. However, if you suddenly need to complete that task within the deadline of one hour, you can probably make it happen.

Here are some examples that put Parkinson's Law into perspective. Think about how much time you spend cleaning out your email inbox (30+ minutes), procrastinating on aversive tasks (weeks), cleaning your guest room (1-2 days), researching possible topics for future projects (4+ hours), or filing the paperwork strewn on your desk (a whole afternoon).

Now, imagine that your email inbox has hit capacity and you

only have 5 minutes to clean it out so you can receive an important email. Or, that the aversive task you've been putting off is suddenly due at 5pm today. Or, that your best friend from out of town just called and they're coming to stay in your guest room this evening. Or, that your boss is holding an emergency meeting in one hour and wants you to pitch your project ideas. Or, that your partner needs to use your office for a video interview in 45 minutes, so you need to file away your paperwork ASAP. Could you do those tasks reasonably well—if not, I dare say, just as well—during the suddenly shortened time period? Yes, most likely, you could. That's Parkinson's Law in action.

Exercise 16:
Determine Timelines with Parkinson's Law

Look back over your list of tasks from Exercise 7. Brainstorm in your notebook or document how much time you would *truly* need to complete the tasks satisfactorily. Then, using Parkinson's Law as your guide, determine whether that "vessel" of time should be longer or shorter, and update your estimated timeframe accordingly. Be honest with yourself and allow wiggle room in case something comes up or you have an "off day."

Boundaries with Technology: Let's Start with Your Phone

Oh, technology. You make my life very happy, with your Pinterest boards of breakfast cookie recipes and motivational quotes on watercolor backgrounds. You keep me up to date on important news. You allow me to set timers for my pulse and pause sessions, chat with friends, have coaching sessions with clients, and write books like this one!

While I am grateful for technology, the more I learn about its addictive nature, the more I decide to set hard boundaries around my usage. I am saying "technology," but to be honest, I am mostly talking about smartphones. I've written multiple blog posts about my experience with my own phone, ranging from taking social media breaks (which resulted in me never loading Twitter back on my phone) or adapting the pulse and pause method to help me stop doomscrolling.[20] These actions were prompted by my growing discomfort with the addictive nature of these often genuinely helpful devices.

The phone itself isn't the issue. The issue is the intermittent reinforcement we receive by repeatedly checking for new follows and likes, and as a result, the hits of dopamine we receive that keep us coming back for more.[21] The issue is reaching for our phones to check our email first thing when we wake up, way before our actual "workday" starts. The issue is falling into a pit of despair and negative self-talk when comparing ourselves to the heavily filtered and stylized photos on influencer accounts. We check these things in bed, in the bathroom, on dates, and alone in our offices when we are procrastinating.

Here are a few methods that have helped me set boundaries around my phone's siren song when I try to focus on work, play, or being present with my loved ones.

- If I'm struggling to stay off social media, I keep social media apps off my phone. I download an app, use it, and then delete it.

- If I catch myself reaching for my phone too often, I put it out of reach. The additional step of choosing to stand up and walk across the room to recover my phone allows me some moments to check if I really want to use my phone.[22]

- I deleted my email app from my phone, which means I need to log in each time via the phone's web browser, and the extra steps required mean that I have more time to decide whether I truly want to check my email.

- I acknowledge that social media's algorithm means that the number of likes, follows, and shares I receive on my posts is arbitrary. That being said, I am especially careful to delete social media from my phone right after I post so that I do not feel tempted to check for updates.

- I keep my phone on silent, and whenever possible, do not disturb. My voicemail recording for my phone literally says, "Hi, this is Kate, and my phone is most likely on silent."

- I use technology blockers on my laptop when I want to do focused writing. I have one that blocks any website I list, and I have one that shuts off my internet access.

- I try to do work by hand whenever possible to take time away from my screen.

- I do not sleep with my phone in my bedroom. Instead, I use a traditional alarm clock.

By no means am I telling you to completely annex your laptop or your phone from your life; instead, I'm inviting you to approach your technology use with more intention, awareness, and control. Exercises 17 and 18 will help you develop more self-awareness around your technology use—specifically your phone.

Exercise 17:
What's Your Relationship with Your Phone?

Before you actually track your technology use, spend some time checking in with your relationship with your phone (you can also write about your relationship with your computer or other tech devices). In your notebook or document, describe your current relationship with your phone. Don't check any screen time trackers to determine how often you use your phone; instead, write about how you feel about your phone (and other technology) usage.

Exercise 18:
Do a Technology Inventory

Step 1: Track Your Technology Use

Spend a few days or a week noticing your relationship with your technology. Pay attention to when you go to pick up your phone—is there a particular cue? Jot down some notes every day about how often/when/how you're using your technology devices (tip: set a pop-up reminder a couple times a day to prompt you to record some notes).

Step 2: Ask Yourself If You Want to Make Changes

At the end of the week, review your notes and your "screen time" data via your phone's settings to see which days you spent the most time on your devices and reflect on why that may have been. Write down answers to the following questions.

- Do you want to delete any apps from your phone or your computer? Why? How will those actions benefit you?

- Do you want to set times when you do not use your technology (e.g., no laptop between 5pm and 9am, no phone between 8pm and 8am, no checking email after 4pm)? Why? How will those actions benefit you?

Step 3: Set Up Accountability

Finally, brainstorm how you will hold yourself accountable for any new changes you'd like to make. If you decide to experiment with new technology boundaries, tell a friend, partner, or roommate and ask them to check in with you about how your new rules are going every week or month.

The Goldilocks Approach to Productivity

This approach is one of the highest return practices that I have developed as a productivity researcher. "Goldilocks and the Three Bears" is a fairytale where a young girl visits the house of a family of bears and tries out the belongings and foods of the mother, father, and baby bear. One option is always lacking, one is too much, but one is ideal, or "just right." For example, the beds are too soft, too hard, or just right. As you can imagine, my method is called the Goldilocks Approach because its success rests on there being an ultimate *just right* approach.

The Goldilocks metaphor is an excellent fit for productivity—especially for projects that lack clear instructions or steps for completion. Like all of my tools, this one is meant to be adapted to *your* personal *just right*, which will vary depending on your project, your task at hand, the amount of time you have for your work session, and the personal resources of energy, focus, and interest that you're bringing to the work session. I'll walk you through the three steps below, and then I'll share prompts for your practice in Exercise 19.

Step 1: Choose A Project and Timeline

To make your own Goldilocks Approach to Productivity, you should choose a project or a task you're working on and predetermine a set timeframe that you'll dedicate to a work session. Determining how much time you have to spend on a work session will help you develop a realistic *just right* goal.

Step 2: Choose Your Goal and Your Not Enough and Too Much

Before you begin your work session, identify an actionable and achievable goal by writing down what would be *not enough* or *too little* and what would be *too much* for you to accomplish in that work session. Consider the time you have to work, your mood, energy, focus levels, and the deadline for your project. Other things that might help you determine what would be *not enough* or *too much* are how much scaffolding and preparation you've already done for this project. Don't set yourself up to do unnecessary labor for this step of the project (remember the Planning Fallacy and Parkinson's Law).

Be honest with yourself when it comes to determining what is *not enough* and *too much*. Think back to times when you failed to achieve your goals, and consider what obstacles caused you to miss your mark. Did you wait until the last minute to work on your project? Did you try to do too much at once, so you ended up feeling defeated and stressed? Allow that awareness to influence what *too much* and *not enough* would look like for your current work session.

If you're still unsure of what to write for *not enough* and *too much*, scale your intention for your larger project down to this single work session and aim to accomplish enough to feel satisfied with your progress. You can do this by considering the total amount of work the larger project will demand and dividing it by how many more work sessions you will have before your final deadline.

Step 3: Identify Your Just Right

Once you've determined what *not enough* and *too much* look like, identify your *just right*. I often ask my coaching clients how a goal feels in their body. How does your *just right* task feel when you check in with yourself? If you feel anxious or overwhelmed or hopeless, experiment with shifting the overwhelming task to your *too much* category, and scale down to create a new *just right*. Repeat this process until you feel engaged and comfortable—even eager—about your goal, and then begin your session.

Here's an example of a Goldilocks Approach to Productivity that would help someone sitting down to start writing a chapter for a book. I put my reasoning for why something is *not enough, just right,* or *too much* in italics, but you do not need to write the reason on your list unless you find it motivating.

Project: Write a First Draft of a Chapter

Time in this Work Session: 2 hours

Not enough: Brainstorm ideas for chapter topic. *This is not enough because it would not make progress on the chapter. Also, I know that I will refine my topic as I read and draft.*

Just right: Identify chapter topic, begin researching the topic online and make a list of articles I might want to read later, and start to draft a chapter outline. *This is just right because I will make real progress on multiple short tasks. Also, I'm setting myself up for success the next time I sit down to write because I will be able to choose to read an article or decide to begin filling in my outline.*

Too much: Read an article and start writing. *This is too much because reading an article may take longer than two hours, and if I start writing without an outline, I won't have a clear focus or purpose.*

Exercise 19:
The Goldilocks Method

Use this activity to plan out your next work session. You can predetermine it now or return to this page when you are gearing up for the work session. I often wait to write my own Goldilocks lists until I sit down to begin a work session.

Step 1: Identify the project you'd like to work on and how long you will be working in your upcoming work session.

Step 2: Identify an actionable and achievable task that you want to complete. Identify what would be *not enough* to move the needle forward during this work session. Identify what would be *too much* to attempt in this work session. Write your *not enough* and *too much* tasks down.

Step 3: Using your *not enough* and *too much* tasks as references, identify what you can actually and efficiently complete during this work session with your current energy and focus levels. This is your *just right* task. Write it between your *not enough* and *too much* items on your list, then display your *not enough*, *just right*, and *too much* list somewhere you can see it while you work. Tip: use "batchotasking" and the pulse and pause method to help you stay on task.

Chapter 5:
A Note on Experimentation

All of the tools, practices, and approaches I have shared in this book are tried and trusted methods for many clients and myself. I have refined them to fit my own life, and I encourage you to do a similar process of trying things on and out, too. I've reserved the final chapter of this book for discussing why I value experimentation as a tenet of developing a personalized productivity toolkit. I also include a how-to guide for experimentation at the end of the chapter.

Why Experimentation?

It is essential to note that experiments with similar tasks will yield different results for different people. When I say "results" here, I mean both the tangible checkmarks on a to-do list *and* the emotional, physical, and mental reactions we have to adding, subtracting, or shifting actions in our daily practices. For readers whose basic needs are generally met due to privilege or access, experimentation with working one day less a week may feel thrilling and generative. For readers who must work multiple jobs to make ends meet while balancing caretaking or other responsibilities, a similar experiment may be insensitive and inaccessible. Therefore, I encourage everyone to approach experimentation with attention to their individual hierarchy of needs being met, prioritizing a better quality of daily life that fits what is accessible to you at this moment.

You can apply the final two exercises in this book to any of the tools and practices that I covered in previous chapters. I'd like to guide you through the process of experimentation that I use and that I teach my coaching clients. To get the most out of Exercise 20, I encourage you to first read through the questions without writing anything, and then I encourage you to fill out your answers in your notebook or document on a second read through.

Exercise 20:
10 Steps for Experimentation

1. Identify a problem you've been trying to fix or a goal you'd like to achieve.

2. Once you have a problem or goal in mind, think about why you haven't accomplished it yet. Some examples are: Is your goal too big/complex? Is the deadline still too far away? Do you feel overwhelmed or confused? Do you need clearer instructions?

3. Identify what a finished project would look like for this goal, and set a deadline for when you'd like to be done. Remember the Planning Fallacy.

4. Identify the steps it would take you to get there and write them in your notebook or document. Then, identify the next best action to take.

5. Using your answers to Steps 1-4 as a guide, choose a tool or approach to practice as you experiment.

6. Choose how long you'll practice (a day, week, month, etc.) to help you act on your next best step (or on the whole project; it's up to you).

7. Check if what you decided to do is actionable and achievable in the timeframe you decided. Adjust the timeframe, tool or approach, or goal for the experiment as needed.

8. Experiment with your practice/approach/tool for the predetermined amount of time.

9. Take notes on your experience throughout the predetermined timeframe for the experiment. What is going well? What isn't going well? How are you measuring "well"? Also, how do you feel about your process?

10. At the end of your experiment, reflect on your experience. What went well? What was fun? What was difficult? What would you change if you used this tool or approach again? If you feel like you "failed" the experiment because you didn't complete your goal, please complete Exercise 21.

Exercise 21:
What If I Didn't Accomplish My Goal?

First of all: it's okay! You are not a failure, and in fact, you DID accomplish your goal of *experimenting*! It's now time to reflect and investigate what the experiment can teach you about what process or action will work best for you moving forward.

Answer the following questions during your end-of-experiment reflection, recording your answers in your notebook or document.

- What got in the way of completing the experiment as you planned? Did you feel scared? Too busy? Did you struggle with a limiting belief? Something else?

- What was your purpose for choosing *that* tool or approach to experiment with for *this* project?

- Would your experiment go differently if you had more (or less) accountability? This could be people you report your progress to, using timers, or posting to a blog or social media about your experiment.

- Should you take something off your plate to give yourself more time/focus/energy to try the experiment again, potentially with a different tool?

- Should you give yourself permission to retry this experiment at a later time?

Finally, regardless of what you feel you did or didn't achieve this time, I *strongly* encourage you to recognize and celebrate what you did accomplish! You read this book, learned and practiced new tools, and set yourself up to find success that lines up with your individual needs, dreams, and inte-rests! Bravo!

Would You Like More Guidance?

I believe approaching a new practice, approach, tool, or goal through the intention of experimentation can take the fear, shame, or sting out of trying new things, which can allow us some much-needed room to grow. Sometimes working with a professional can help streamline that process. If you enjoyed the exercises in this book, consider booking a one-on-one Productivity Coaching session with me. As of Winter/ Spring 2021, I am currently accepting clients for two offerings, but you should check my website for my most recent list of offerings.

Single Session Slowductivity Coaching includes a one-hour coaching session where we will cover one or two questions or goals you have.

Success & Accountability Mentorship is available in 3-month and 6-month package options. This includes a pre-session question-naire, monthly one-hour coaching session, detailed and confidential notes that include explicit deadlines and a to-do list, weekly accounta-bility email check-ins from me, and an additional half-hour coaching call at the end of month three (3-month package) and months three and six (6-month package).

You can learn more about these offerings, read client testimo-nials, check my current rates, and book a session with me at <u>theten-dingyear.com/work-with-me</u>. You can contact me with any questions or comments at <u>thetendingyear@gmail.com</u>.

All my best wishes,
   Dr. Kate Litterer

Suggested Resources

This is a list of resources that I have found helpful in my own personal productivity journey.

Podcasts:
- adrienne maree brown's interview on the *Hurry Slowly Podcast*: https://hurryslowly.co/304-adrienne-maree/
- Tricia Hersey's interview on the *For the Wild* podcast: https://forthewild.world/listen/tricia-hersey-on-rest-as-resistance-185
- *Letters from a Hopeful Creative* with Sara Tasker and Jen Carrington
- *Here to Thrive* with Kate Snowise
- *The Slow Home Podcast* with Brooke McAlary
- *The DIY Small Business Podcast* with Yarrow Magdalena

Books:
- Jenny Odell's *How to Do Nothing: Resisting the Attention Economy*
- Marlee Grace's *How to Not Always Be Working: A Toolkit for Creativity and Radical Self-Care*
- Leah Lakshmi Piepzna-Samarasinha's *Care Work: Dreaming Disability Justice*
- Melissa Gregg's *Counterproductive: Time Management in the Knowledge Economy*
- Sarah Knight's *Get Your Shit Together*

- Chris Bailey's *The Productivity Project*
- Gretchen Rubin's *Better than Before*

Instagram Accounts:
- The Nap Ministry @thenapministry
- Bunny Michael @bunnymichael
- France Corbel @traitspourtraits
- Yumi Sakugawa @yumisakugawa
- Morgan Harper Nichols @morganharpernichols
- Rachel Cargle @rachel.cargle

Newsletters:
- Anne Helen Peterson's "Culture Study": https://annehelen.substack.com/
- Jen Carrington's "Weekly Letters": http://www.jencarrington.com/
- Hadassah Damien's "Ride Free Fearless Money": https://www.ridefreefearlessmoney.com/

Applications:
- Pulse and Pause Method timers: Freedom, BeFocused, Tomato Timer, Forest, MindHero
- Todoist (digital to-do list)
- Internet blockers: Freedom for computers and phones, StayFocused for Google Chrome, Pause for Google Chrome

About the Author

Dr. Kate Litterer is a Productivity Coach, independent researcher, and author who lives outside Boston, Massachusetts, United States. Dr. Litterer received her MFA degree in Creative Writing and her Master's degree and Doctoral degree in Rhetoric and Composition from the University of Massachusetts Amherst. Her writing has been published by A-Minor Press, *The Journal of Lesbian Studies*, *The Homeworker*, *The Temper*, *GradHacker*, and numerous online and print journals. You can reach Dr. Litterer directly via the contact form on thetendingyear.com.

Notes

[1] You can listen to all podcast interviews with Kate at www.theten-dingyear.com/aboutkate.

[2] To hear more about my personal connection of alcoholism and workaholism, read my article for The Temper, "How Recovering From Alcohol Use Disorder Helped Me Recognize My Workaholism," at www.thetemper.com/workaholism.

[3] To learn more about how white supremacy influences work culture, read Showing Up for Racial Justice's "The Characteristics of White Supremacy Culture" at www.showingupforracialjustice.org/white-supre-macy-culture-characteristics.

[4] You can read more about the process of emotional connection to goals at http://www.lifehack.org/articles/featured/the-science-of-setting-goals.

[5] You can read more about the "ideal fill-in-the-black" approach in one of my first blog posts, "Three Keys to Abundance," via the link www.thetendingyear.com/1-2-three-keys-to-abundance.

[6] It is not lost on me that I am releasing this book during a global pandemic, which means working for six hours at a public coffee shop is unfortunately not possible and likely won't be for a while (at least in the U.S.).

[7] You can read more about how why and how some chronically ill people use Spoon Theory to communicate their experiences in my blog post "Spoon Theory: What It Is and How I Use It" at the link www.theten-

dingyear.com/2-30-spoon-theory-what-it-is-how-i-use-it.

[8] You can learn more about the psychology of habit formation at www.psychologytoday.com/us/basics/habit-formation.

[9] You can learn more about Rubin' take on habit formation at www.gretchenrubin.com/books/better-than-before/about-the-book.

[10] You can read more about setting intentions in "How to Live with Intention Using Values + Presence" at www.thetendingyear.com/1-27-how-to-live-with-intention-using-values-presence.

[11] To learn more about the ties between work obsession and institutionalized racism and white supremacy, listen to Tricia Hersey's *For the Wild* podcast interview at www.forthewild.world/listen/tricia-hersey-on-rest-as-resistance-185.

[12] You can read more about using a "why" or purpose in "Have Purpose on Purpose" at www.thetendingyear.com/1-45-have-purpose-on-purpose.

[13] You can read more about procrastination at www.alifeofproductivity.com/why-you-procrastinate-10-tactics-to-help-you-stop.

[14] You can read a definition of "batch" at www.merriam-webster.com/dictionary/batch.

[15] You can learn more about monotasking at www.alifeofproductivity.com/do-one-thing-at-a-time/.

[16] You can read my article about all of the productivity practices that

helped me finish my dissertation at www.insidehighered.com/blogs/gradhacker/5-productivity-practices-helped-me-finish-my-dissertation.

[17] You can access the BeFocused timer by searching for "BeFocused" on whatever app platform you use.

[18] You can access the Forest timer at www.forestapp.cc/.

[19] You can read more about workaholism and graduate school in my blog posts "Workaholic Tendencies" at www.thetendingyear.com/1-23-workaholic-tendencies and "The Recovering Workaholic's Guide to Taking Breaks" at www.thetendingyear.com/2-3-the-recovering-workaholics-guide-to-taking-breaks.

[20] You can read about my experiments with phone boundaries at "Mindful Consumption" at www.thetendingyear.com/1-4-mindful-consumption.

[21] I know that I keep mentioning dopamine. I'm definitely not anti-dopamine; rather, I encourage us all to acknowledge the ways dopamine serves as an invisible reward for routines we may not acknowledge are habits.

[22] I recently heard tech researcher Nicholas Carr tell Ezra Klein in an interview that even having our phone in the room with us makes it difficult to focus. You can read an excerpt of their conversation and listen to that podcast at www.vox.com/podcasts/2020/7/1/21308153/the-ezra-klein-show-the-shallows-twitter-facebook-attention-deep-reading-thinking.